CREATIVE THINKING:

What Top Creative People From Around the World Can Teach Us

By

K.A. DeWolf

Introduction

Thank you for purchasing the book, *"Creative Thinking: What Top Creative People From Around The World Can Teach Us"*.

As a creative person, when you think of success, there are a myriad of role models at whom you can look up to. No matter what you're interested in, there is a corresponding creative who is a master in that field. The key is to study what and how you can learn from these creative people.

In this book, we will examine the top **twenty most creative thinkers in the world** today. We'll take a brief look at who they are and what they do. Don't miss the last chapter when we put together a list of the top twenty-five lessons we can learn from these creative thinkers.

It's my sincere desire that you take it a step further than that. I hope you are inspired to focus on ways that you can become a creative thinker. The world is the wonderful place it is today because of people like you who decided to affect positive change.

Thanks again for purchasing this book, I hope you enjoy it!

TABLE OF CONTENT

Chapter 1: Advocates for the Underdog

Because this wonderful world we live in is made up of amazing individuals, many people miss out on chances based on societal biases and stereotypes.

In some situations, this also entails lifting up those who are **less advantaged** due to location and social class. This chapter will examine creative people who have dedicated their lives to finding these amazing people and advancing their station.

Vikram Vora, CEO and CoFounder of MyDentist

Vikram worked as a salesman of dental equipment in the late 2000's. As he traveled from clinic to clinic, he noticed how disgruntled the customers were with the wait times, pricing, and shoddy equipment. Vikram began to consider what would improve this obviously unsuccessful, but necessary, business model.

In 2010, he launched MyDentist. Vikram based his new dental clinics on a cafe model. Patients were presented with low fixed prices on procedures, predetermined waiting times, and up-to-date equipment. Needless to say, this was well-received by the working class who were unable to be served by the previous model. The main factor of which was cost and time constraints.

In a little over three years, Vikram's idea has expanded to seventy-two clinics serving the working class all across Mumbai, India. By setting up his clinics around the commuter train stations in Mumbai, Vikram has met the people right where they are. The clinics are also interchangeable in that any procedure can be completed at any one of them. For example, if a dental implant is initiated at a location close to a patients' home, but convenient for them to complete at a clinic close to their job, this is indeed possible and a seamless process.

Vikram has accomplished something that is not happening **anywhere else in the world**. His company employs 280 full-time dentists and dental assistants, as well as 120 consultants who all come from working class families and have been trained by the company.

The lesson we can learn from Vikram is to solve problems by ascertaining where there is a need in your community and then fulfilling that need at an amazing level.

Princess Reema Bint Bandar Al-Saud, CEO of Alfa Intl.

A princess and a creative thinker, Princess Reema understood that only half of people in Saudi Arabia were employed in the workforce. The half that were unemployed consisted entirely of women. Saudi Arabia is known to be one of the least progressive nations in the world, and inviting women into the workforce was unheard of. Traditionalists see this as a radical act.

In the last two years, Princess Reema has **empowered women** in her company, Alfa Intl., which is a luxury retailer in Saudi Arabia. She has gone so far as to replace experienced salesmen with women. New laws were passed by the Saudi government to regulate the areas where men were able to work in the retail sector. For example, men were banned from working in lingerie and cosmetic shops that only served female customers. This created new areas for female employment.

Princess Reema is the daughter of Prince Bandar, a long-time ambassador for Saudi Arabia in the United States. As a result, she grew up in Washington D.C. Yet she holds now that she is back home that she is not seeking to Westernize her country, but evolve it into more modern ideals.

Even though Princess Reema was planning to spend some time as a stay-at-home mother, the Harvey Nichols store run by her company in her hometown of Riyadh was in dire need of renovation.

This resulted in a complete gutting of the location and making accommodations for her workforce of women. The company provided transportation since most Saudi women are forbidden to drive cars. They also allowed for childcare on site to help workers battle the "who's going to watch the children" argument.

As a result, Princess Reema has not been free of **backlash** in her city of Riyadh. The Harvey Nichols store location, also the first to open outside of the United Kingdom, has experienced a 42% drop in revenue. This is due in part to the high volume of women employed as well as a boycott by those loyal to the aforementioned experienced salesmen. Still Princess Reema is confident that the social perception will change.

From Princess Reema we can learn that social change must happen and can be initiated by the empowerment of people who are wrongly perceived to be inferior.

Catherine Hoke, Founder and CEO of Defy Ventures

How can we take possibly the most looked-down on people of American society and exalt them to greatness and self-sufficiency? It is a daunting undertaking, but Catherine Hoke has proved that it's possible. According to a study conducted in 2005, nearly 68% of state prisoners who were released were rearrested within three years. That number skyrocketed to nearly 77% within five years.

The harsh truth is that people who are released from prison have very little opportunities when they get out. As a marked felon, jobs are difficult to come by, and those that are obtainable are usually minimum wage positions. Former thieves and drug dealers have a hard time with this reality and often return to a life a crime.

Catherine had an **epiphany** after touring Texas prisons in 2004. She noticed how criminals organized themselves within their crime circles much like a corporation is set up. She decided to come up with a way to put those skills to use legally. The skills were already there, they were just being used for the wrong reasons.

Catherine started an entrepreneurship program in the Texas prison system. Upon moving to New York, she founded Defy Ventures and developed a six-month program that teaches former inmates the basics of starting their own company. The participants are involved in **business plan competitions** and are catapulted into a three-month incubator period to see their ideas come to fruition.

Since it started, Defy Ventures has produced 115 graduates. Seventy-one of those graduates have gone on to create their own companies. So what's next for Defy Ventures? Catherine plans to take the program national and help former inmates all across the United States.

Catherine teaches us that finding the right solution for people that society has been unable to help is a win-win for America. Not only does she employ the unemployable, she indirectly creates additional jobs in the economy.

(Sources: **http://www.nij.gov/topics/corrections/recidivism/Pa ges/welcome.aspx**)

Jose Maria Alvarez-Pallete, Founder of Wayra; Coo, Telefonica S.A.

In 2010, Jose traveled through the Silicon Valley in California. He was amazed at how many **Latin-American** programmers and designers he met on his trip. This left him with a question. Why did they have to relocate to America to be successful in the tech industry? This left his company, Telefonica, having to order supplies and software from abroad.

A creative person like Jose only requires being presented with a need before coming up with a fantastic solution. He knew that in order for his company to grow, the surrounding tech economy would have to grow as well. In 2011, Jose launched his idea called Wayra, a South American native word meaning wind. Within six months, Wayra was up and running. By the end of its first year, it had academies set up in seven countries across the globe.

Wayra received a boost in 2013 to the tune of $13.4 million from Jose's other company, Telefonica. It now boasts 14 academies and has reached a milestone as one of the **world's largest accelerators** of start ups in less than two years.

Jose saw that he could build an ecosystem for his own endeavors while accelerating others in an area that required people to leave their country to succeed.

Chapter 2: Advancing the Internet and Mobile Web

Computers have become an integral part of our lives as have mobile devices. We are constantly digitally connected to a web that gives us access to almost the entire world at any given moment.

This is the result of some of the most creative thinkers of all time. Even so, the **Internet and Mobile Web** have created a platform on which an entire generation of creatives will make their fortunes. Here's what we can learn from them for those of you who are more technically inclined.

Michael Heyward, Founder and CEO of Whisper

We are currently going through a period when privacy and anonymity are sacred thoughts. Into an online world where it seems every avenue wants to share your data comes the likes of Whisper. Whisper is a mobile app where users can confess their secrets under the veil of anonymity. Like sitting down in the confessional with millions of priests who don't know who you are.

Michael Heyward developed Whisper to keep digital trails coming to dead ends. Users type out a secret and overlay it on a relevant image. The content is then added to a database served to millions of other users everyday. Whisper doesn't have user profiles or a platform to follow other users. Communication is had via private anonymous messages or by posting one's own secret in response to another. The big deal here is being able to remain completely anonymous if that's what you want.

So what application boasts 3.5 billion page views a month surpassing the New York Times website for a whole quarter? That's right, Whisper.

Michael Heyward shows us that we can battle unwanted intrusions on any level with a simple rebuttal...even with a whisper.

Sean Rad and Justin Mateen, CoFounders of Tinder

Sometimes innovation isn't about creating a new concept, but rather simplifying an existing idea.

Online dating is huge, but Sean and Justin wanted to find a way to make it less complicated. Traditional online dating sites involve filling out an extensive profile and answering a ton of questions in order to be matched with potential love interests. While this model has worked for millions, it isn't for everyone. The profiles are often so extensive, they don't leave much to be discussed during the "get to know you" phase of dating. Also, those who aren't inclined toward detailed communication are left wondering about a lot of things.

Tinder is a mobile app that took the dating site profile down to a single image and reduced initial communication to a simple swipe of the thumb: Right for yea and left for nay. Justin says this interface "captures the moment when your eyes connect with someone." It brings that aspect of meeting someone face to face into a digital setting.

Users of the app are guaranteed of mutual attraction since Tinder only notifies them if both parties swipe right. There has been great success with this simplicity with 10 million matches and **750 million** swipes by users on a daily basis. Sean and Justin have plans to develop the app further with more fun and light-hearted features in the near future.

Tim Kendall, Head of Product at Pinterest

You don't have to be Internet and Social Media savvy to know that Pinterest is huge. What you may not know is if your business is geared toward women and you are considering Pinterest, it would be a very savvy move. Why? Because 80% of Pinterest users are **women** and they produce 92% of the items pinned. Pinterest also has demonstrated its influence to markets both online and off. Cha-ching!

So where does Tim Kendall come into play on all of this? As the Head of Product at Pinterest, Tim was instrumental in launching the Pinterest app for the iPhone, Android and tablets in 2013. It wasn't just the release of the apps though, it was the fact that apps allowed pins to display more information to mobile users. This rocketed Pinterest traffic and 75% of that traffic now comes from a mobile device.

Tim took something that worked, made it better, and then made it portable thereby adding tremendous value to an already huge company.

(Source for Pinterest stats: **http://marketingland.com/report-92-percent-pinterest-pins-made-women-83394**)

Alan Schaaf, Founder of Imgur

Content is king of the Internet. In the past, that content referred mainly to written content. Once the power of images were realized on a number of levels such as marketing, engagement and entertainment, they became a staple as well. It's not enough just to be able to use images online, but **sharing images** is also widely popular.
Even with Social Media dominating the web, old mediums are still popular like message boards, forums, and social bookmarking sites like Reddit.com. Most of these platforms don't allow space for image uploading. Enter an image host like Imgur.

Alan has gone to great lengths to ensure that Imgur is the leading image host on the net. It's packed with features and allows commenting and private messaging between users. In addition, users who just want to unwind can use the site without logging in and view images by just clicking the Next button.

Imgur boasts **130 million unique hits** per month as a treasure chest of viral images and memes. It's basically a social network for image sharing. Alan's innovation has made Imgur one of the most popular sites on the Internet.

Alan teaches us that you can use the same idea as someone else and make it something great by making it better. He's paid attention to the evolution of Imgur and shaped the site to fit how its audience uses it.

Chapter 3: Innovations in Creative Renewal

Whether your idea of renewal is upcycling, making something old new again, or something completely different, there is no doubt that renewal of any kind takes innovation and creativity. The stories in this chapter will no doubt warm your heart and perhaps inspire you in a little creative renewal of your own.

Roger Norris Gordon, CoFounder and President of Food Cowboy

Forty-three billion pounds of food rot in garbage dumps each year because it gets bruised or damaged on the way to local grocers. If you consider **world hunger** rates, this is ludicrous. Roger wasn't willing to let it happen. Of course the delivery of this food to those in need is too expensive an endeavor for the companies shipping the produce.

What did Roger do? He jumped on his computer and helped his brother and many other truck drivers find a home for their unwanted loads at shelters close to the truckers' locations. Then he started thinking about **Mobile technology** and how most, if not all, trucks have smart phones. This could make the ease of finding a location for their damaged, but still edible haul as simple as sending a text message.

In 2012, Food Cowboy was born. Roger and his brother founded the company which is essentially a web application that allows truckers to be matched to local shelters where they can drop unwanted food. The food gets into needy hands and is kept out of the garbage dump. Hundreds of **truckers** have signed up. Together they have saved more than 500,000 pounds of food. This has garnered attention from the U.S. Department of Agriculture who hopes an expo on the subject will bring more ideas like Roger's.

Roger recognized a need and filled it with a waste. In so doing, though, he stopped a shameful waste of life-giving food.

Michael Phillips Moskowitz, Chief Curator at eBay

In 1995, eBay was founded in a San Jose living room. Since then, it has been an Internet staple. You would probably be hard-pressed to find an avid Internet user who doesn't have a log in for this giant online yard sale. Since its inception, it has grown and evolved over the years, but managed to maintain the model with which it began.

Secondhand shoppers are no longer limited to local shops. They can shop the world for treasures among another person's unwanted items.

So, what could be better? Michael found a way to highlight the coolest items he and his team found through the medium of **curation**. Content curation is just a fancy term for organizing content in a list or under a specific theme and presenting it in a meaningful way. Anyone with an eBay log in can access Michael and his team's collections like "**Retro Redux**" or "**The Natural World**".

Michael's collections are more than just lists. Michael focuses on the story and retells that story as a part of every collection he puts together. It's the story that sells the items and brings millions of users looking for his lists. He creates a meaningful experience to accompany each item he curates and that's what sells merchandise.

Michael's recognition that the story is just as important as the items connects with an audience who feels the same way. This personal connection makes Michael's creative renewal innovation a success!

(Sources:http://www.cs.brandeis.edu/~magnus/ief2 48a/eBay/history.html)

Billy Parish, CoFounder and President of Mosaic

When it comes to fossil fuels and clean energy, there is a lot of controversy. As people, we recognized long ago that we needed to let go of fossil fuels and move on to cleaner, **renewable energy** sources. This transition has yet to happen; however, with advocates like Billy Parish, we will begin to see such changes happen more quickly.

Billy is fully aware that the reason our transition to clean energy is so slow is because fossil fuels generate a staggering amount of revenue for fuel companies. When he launched Mosaic in 2013, he asserted that "The shift from fossil fuels to **clean energy** represents one of the largest wealth-creation opportunities of our time, if we can democratize ownership of the assets."

That's exactly what Billy sought to do with Mosaic. It's actually a crowd-funding platform that connects investors with solar projects that are under-financed. Anyone who has as little as $25 to spend, can invest. This has produced $7 million for commercial projects, but Billy hasn't stopped there. In early 2014, Mosaic began **funding loans** for residences too.

Billy broke down our hesitation, found a solution, and moved forward to innovate in the much-needed area of renewable energy. The Earth will thank him one day.

Theaster Gates, Artist, Founder of Rebuild Project, and the Director of Arts and Public Life at the University of Chicago

What do you get when you mix art with a taste for good culture? The answer is Theaster Gates. Theaster started at a residential level on the South Side of Chicago when he needed a place to live in 2006. He has transformed empty homes into **cultural spaces**. He also turned a former housing project into residences and a hub for the arts.

Theaster's latest project is the transformation of an old bank building into a library that will house an archive of African-American history. In addition, it will also include a restaurant. This will provide for a significant need on the South and West sides for a place to get a drink and a nice meal.

At the same time, Theaster is also tackling a giant art project for the Chicago Transit Authority. Rather than lock into a specific theme for the project, Theaster has partnered with area radio stations to create content to inspire residents to think outside the box about what kind of art this project should include. Theaster concludes that by doing so, he will foster artistic leadership rather just artistic production.

Theaster has sought to include culture in the public space in a big way because he knows that culture should be central to how the human landscape functions.

Chapter 4: Taking Entertainment Forward in a New Age

With the onset of so many avenues to create, entertainment isn't just about television, radio, and music anymore. A large expansion has taken place in the last decade that has presented the Internet and mobile devices as big players in the entertainment game. A marriage with **traditional media** has made this content streamable to Smart TV's, cell phones, computers, and tablets. Everything is a crossover these days and we'll talk about innovations in entertainment in this chapter.

King Bach, Comedian

The cool thing about the Internet and entertainment are all of the platforms that pop up from ideas and take off. Like building a piano and finding someone who plays by ear, these platforms just resonate with some people. They have a knack for appealing to raw talent. It's always astonishing to find those people who have taken an instrument or platform and mastered it.

Andrew Bachelor has more than **9 million followers** on the popular video platform, Vine. What is amazing is that he's gained that following in just over a year under his user name **King Bach**. He's used the six-second time limit to establish himself as a comedic force. A month after his Vine debut, he had a million followers and a deal with United Talent Agency.

Andrew isn't stopping there. He's used Vine to catapult his career into television. He's a regular on Showtime's *House of Lies*. He is also working on an upcoming project with Adult Swim and has caught the attention of several other comedians. His gigantic success on Vine led him on to television and made him a major player in the evolution of entertainment.

Andrew tried something new, found he had a knack for it, and rode his raw talent into huge success that is just beginning for this young man.

Jenji Kohan, Creator of Orange Is The New Black

Netflix. Need we say more? The mail DVD rental company turned streaming video service has subscribers in the tens of millions. The numbers give long-established cable premium channels like HBO a run for their money. In 2011, Netflix set it sights on creating original content, and by 2013, had hit paydirt with *House of Cards*. It couldn't get much better, or could it?

Enter Jenji Kohan and her creation *Orange Is The New Black*. The show premiered in the Summer of 2013 without too many expectations. Jenji was just having fun since she was already the **creator** of Showtime's *Weeds*, a moderately successful venture of a show about marijuana.

So what could Jenji do with a New York backdrop, a cast of new talent, and some creative writing? The result was a huge surprise hit in *Orange Is The New Black*. It's a melding of drama and comedy in the setting of a womens' prison. Jenji sought out under-utilized talent for the female-dominent roles. She then set about writing a show that she found entertaining, and in so doing has delighted millions.

Netflix is notorious for not releasing numbers such as viewership, but Gigaom.com reported that more than **60 million** people have pirated episodes of the series using peer-to-peer networks. Needless to say, Jenji's masterpiece was renewed for a second and third season so far. She's braced herself for the pressure and says she's just trying to "make the best show possible".

Jenji took a concept, fleshed it out with lesser known actors, and turned it into an overnight sensation proving great things come to those who give talent a chance.

Sources: **http://en.wikipedia.org/wiki/Netflix https://gigaom.com/2014/08/20/orange-is-the-new-black-torrent-statistics/**

Tim and Karrie League, CoFounder of Alamo Drafthouse

Let's not forget the Silver Screen. From our previous write up involving Netflix, it's obvious that movie rentals are still a viable industry. However, it's not just being able to watch at home. **Theaters** are also still viable members of the movie industry as a whole. They've been the same for decades; head to the theater, buy a ticket, maybe get some popcorn, and watch the latest films from Hollywood.

So, how might one go about broadening the movie experience? Why, include adult beverages and a meal of course! That's exactly what Tim and Karrie have done with their Alamo Drafthouse. It wasn't enough to just create the venue though, they also have a film distribution company called Drafthouse Films. You might be inclined to think that these endeavors wouldn't succeed without the glitz of Hollywood or all the latest films. You would be wrong.

Tim and Karrie have taken the Alamo nationwide and opened eight more theaters in 2013 bring their total to seventeen. They hope to have fifty theaters operating by 2017. They're not just branching out though. In 2013, Drafthouse Films' The Act of Killing was nominated for an Oscar. They also host an annual film festival which is one of the largest in the U.S. called Fantastic Fest. They hosted the debut of Forever Fest in Austin which emphasizes programming created by women for women.

Tim is known for his **unorthodox publicity** methods as well. He promoted Drafthouse Films by challenging the director, producer, and star to have a bit of a beer drink-off to see who wet themselves first. Tim lost. He has also been widely publicized for his ban on Madonna due to her headline debacle when she was called out for texting during a screening of 12 Years A Slave. It seems Tim is a bit of an advocate for proper moving-going etiquette.

Tim and Karrie took a tried and true entertainment venue and made it phenomenal. Their gamble paid off big time and proves they are in a "League" of their own.

Mario Queiroz, VP of Product Management, Google

For decades, televisions have required a helping hand usually in the form of a set-top box of some sort. In the late 2000's, the era of the antenna finally bowed to this model. Whether you're a cable and satellite subscriber, or subscribe to nothing in particular, odds are that you have some type of **extraneous box** plugged into your television. Consumers scrambled when SmartTV's hit the market.

A SmartTV included the ability to access streaming services like Netflix, Hulu, Amazon, and even YouTube without requiring yet one more box.
One man brought the $200 billion SmartTV industry to its knees when he introduced a small solution at just $35 a pop. Mario Queiroz took all the added functionality of a SmartTV and crammed it in the **Google Chromecast**, a small dongle that fits into the HDMI port on most modern televisions. At such an affordable price, the Chromecast was a more practical solution than buying a new television.

Mario stopped the SmartTV revolution with a simple device that has sold millions. Meanwhile, we are all waiting for the next big thing in television. However, in the meantime, we can enjoy a plethora of streaming services as well as being able to "cast" streaming web content from the likes of YouTube, Pandora, and many other popular services.

Mario and his team at Google took just eighteen months to take the Chromecast from a concept to market. He came up with a better solution to the problem than a whole new television and he packaged it small with a price tag that packed incredible value. Amazing!

Chapter 5: New Discoveries in Science and Medicine

If mankind were to stop advancing in Science and Medicine, would we go on? It's not likely. Creativity is not merely reserved for the Arts and Entertainment. Every realm of our culture and being requires creative thinking. This book would not be complete without a chapter to highlight some very important players who are innovating in the very important fields of Science and Medicine.

Jorge Odon, Inventor of the Odon Device

Sometimes solutions come from the most unlikely of places. Can you imagine a man with no medical training developing a device to ease childbirth in developing countries? That's exactly what Jorge did. His invention began with a problem as most do. Of the deaths that occur to mothers in childbirth, 99% of them are due to lack of training for doctors and lack of proper equipment all in developing countries.

The next phase of Jorge's epiphany was the result of a rather random issue. In 2006, Jorge was working as an auto mechanic and watched his co-workers demonstrate how to remove a cork from a bottle using a plastic bag, which they learned of all places, from a **YouTube video**. Later that night, Jorge woke with the idea: wouldn't this concept work if the bottle were a uterus and the cork was a baby to assist in childbirth?

Jorge went to work and made a glass uterus filled with one of his daughter's dolls. He took the idea to a Buenes Aires teaching hospital where it was received with open arms. People at the hospital helped him apply for the patents he would need and by Jorge's birthday on March 1, 2011, thirty live trials were launched by he and his team. They were all successful. In 2014, Jorge left his job as a mechanic to further develop the Odon device full-time as research continues worldwide.

Jorge took a random idea and developed it into a device to solve a completely unrelated problem. That is definitely the result of some creative thinking and shows that sometimes, people develop amazing products outside of their chosen field.

Chase Adam, CoFounder and CEO of Watsi

There's always more work to do in the developing world. Medicine is one of the largest fields in need of more people and more innovation. The fact that people in these countries receive second-class care or even die for lack of funds, knowledge, or equipment is absurd in the modern world. Chase Adam is among the people making that a less common occurrence.

Chase is focused on finding the **high-benefit, low-risk** areas where creativity can happen with the medical field. Otherwise it can be a touchy subject with privacy issues and other factors coming into play. Chase believes that putting more emphasis of the user experience in the **healthcare industry** will take the industry leaps and bounds. While there has been a lot of focus on the business to business of the industry, little innovation has happened in the patient realm.

So what is Chase doing as his part to make these ideas a reality? He developed Watsi which is a platform for crowd-funding. It allows users to donate directly to people seeking medical treatment in developing countries. Chase has taken a small piece of the puzzle and put it into place to solve the problem of money for people who otherwise would go without proper treatment.

Chase started with a small area and created a solution to one huge problem. There's no doubt he's working on the next one as this is being written.

Carl Hart, Neuroscientist at Columbia University

Drug abuse and addiction has been a serious problem for a long time, but is addiction really as strong as we think? Carl Hart doesn't think so. He conducted and published a study in 2012 that showed **meth addicts** would almost always choose $20 over a hit of meth. Carl has also done research that leans toward drug addiction being the result of environment rather than brain impulse as commonly thought.

Carl thinks that the term, addiction, is used on too wide a scale and has gone on record against government representatives. He's gone to bat against discrepancies in science and policies that often put the underprivileged at a disadvantage. Carl draws from his experience growing up in a rough **Miami neighborhood** in holding that scientists tend to characterize drug addicts and drug takers in stark contrast to what he witnessed growing up.

Carl isn't willing to let trends in science dictate the science behind experience. His research and stance on drug abuse research deserves applause.

Kathryn Hunt, Paleo-Oncologist

What if you found yourself freshly returned home from an expedition in Egypt when you found out that you were suffering from **ovarian cancer**? That happened to Kathryn Hunt. Now in remission, she began putting together the pieces shortly after that expedition. Many of the bones she was studying had evidence of disease. Then there was the ancient record which mentioned cancer repeatedly. There was no concrete evidence because there was a lack of clarity on what cancer in ancient remains would look like.

Kathryn and a few of her colleagues founded the Paleo-Oncology Research Organization and have since identified more than 230 cases of likely cancer in ancient societies. As a result, they have put together an open-source database for researchers to discuss and share information.

In the future, Kathryn is aiming to acquire funding to study some of those cases more deeply with radiological analysis, as well as, DNA testing. She hopes to be able to identify patterns in the ancient record and give researchers areas on which to focus more intently.

Kathryn put two and two together as a result of her own adversity and made breakthroughs in the study of ancient societies and Medicine.

Chapter 6: The Top 25 Lessons You Can Learn From the Most Creative People in the World

1. Problems are solved most often by identifying a need in your community, and fulfilling that need.

2. Empowering the seemingly inferior people in a culture will promote societal changes.

3. Employing people that society deems unemployable creates positive trends in the economy and indirectly creates additional job opportunities for others.

4. When focusing on business expansion, expand your surrounding business ecosystem at the same time to ensure longevity.

5. Sometimes fighting back against significant intrusions or attack on a personal or business level need only be rebutted with a whisper.

6. You don't have to create something new to innovate. You can innovate by simplifying an existing idea.

7. Don't be afraid to expand on ideas that are already working well. You have the potential of making it better.

8. Success doesn't always come from new ideas. Sometimes you can succeed by taking an existing idea and making it better.

9. When providing a service to people, constantly shape your service to the way your audience uses it.

10. Seek ways to fulfill needs with resources that would otherwise be wasted.

11. Remember that the story is just as important as the sale.

12. Always seek to connect with people on a personal level.

13. If money is a barrier to a new innovation, find a way to make it profitable.

14. Do not hesitate.

15. Include culture in everything you create. The human landscape should always reflect heritage and functionality.

16. Try everything. If you have a knack for something, do it a lot.

17. Be careful not to ignore your own raw talent. Feed it.

18. Utilize talent because it's talent, not because there's a name attached to it.
19. Expand on tradition. Make it new while preserving the old.
20. Solve problems by including more value and smaller price tags. The fortune will be the same.
21. If you ignore random ideas, you might miss out on an amazing innovation.
22. Innovation can happen for you outside of your chosen field.
23. Start small. Sometimes the smallest ideas solve the largest problems.
24. Do not ignore your own experience no matter what others say. Rely on it.
25. Adversity can be the greatest teacher. Listen to what it's trying to say and learn from it.

Conclusion

There you have it. What did you learn from the top twenty most creative people in the world? What stood out to you the most? There's quite a range of people from all walks of life.

Remember how your parents told you that you could be anything you wanted when you were growing up? This is what they were talking about. These people are living proof that you can be anything and that anyone can be an innovator.

Don't stop here! Take those twenty-five lessons and start finding ways to fit them into your life. You might just find yourself on the next top twenty list of creative thinkers with a few lessons of your own to share.

Finally, if you enjoyed this book, then I'd like to ask you for a favor, would you be kind enough to leave a review for this book on Amazon? It'd be greatly appreciated!

Thank you and good luck!

K.A. DeWolf

Check Out My Other Books:

Memory Improvement:: 25 Powerful Ways to Improve Your Memory in 30 Days

Bullying: Stop Bullying; Effective Ways To Overcome Bullying In School Permanently: Modern Day Approach To Prevent Bullying Once And For All

Bootstrapping Entrepreneur: 100 Free Online Tools for Startups and First-Time Entrepreneurs: Small Business Tools For Entrepreneur Startup, Small Business Ideas, Online Tools for Business

Learn How to Use a Computer: 50 Tips and Suggestions to Help You Get the Most Out of Your Computer

Creative Thinking: What Top Creative People From Around The World Can Teach Us

Dog Sense: Top Lessons in Learning Dog Behavior and Understanding Your Dog
Getting Things Done: Mastering Productivity by Getting Your Habits and Routines Under Control

Dog Training: 30-Day Train Your Dog Guide for Becoming a Great Companion: Obedience Training and Learning Amazing Tricks

Make Money Live Happy: How To Make A Living Doing What You Love: 25 Lessons From 25 Most Successful Entreprenuers From Around The World

Dyslexia In Children: Guide To Identity, Manage and Overcome Dyslexia: 25 Powerful Tips and Suggestions To Empower You Dyslexic Child

Insecurity: Stop Being Insecure and Develop Your Confidence and Self Esteem Today

50 Brain Training Strategies: Incredible Brain Training Strategies To Help You Increate Your Mind Power, Concentration, Mental Clarity and Neuroplasticity

FREE Kindle Books and New Kindle Book Announcements!

Join our exclusive readers club and receive notification when our books are FREE on Kindle Store for limited time. Also be the first to know about exciting new titles that are published every month for only $0.99.

*** We hate spam and never share your email with anyone ***

JOIN NOW!

Visit this link:
http://bit.ly/1AtBHOU

www.ingramcontent.com/pod-product-compliance
Lightning Source LLC
Chambersburg PA
CBHW070744180526
45168CB00004B/1532